THE CAPITALIST PARTY MANIFESTO

Defects within our democracy and what we can do to change it!

Christopher Morrall

First published in Great Britain by Hansib Publications in 2020

Hansib Publications Limited
P.O. Box 226, Hertford, SG14 3WY

info@hansibpublications.com
www.hansibpublications.com

ISBN 978-1-912662-17-3
ISBN 978-1-912662-25-8 (Kindle)
ISBN 978-1-912662-26-5 (ePub)

A CIP catalogue record for this book
is available from the British Library

Design & Production by Hansib Publications Ltd

Printed in Great Britain

As with all other great human endeavours and achievements; advances in the sciences and engineering, industry and communications, technology and healthcare, we may at last put the same effort and resources into improving politics.

Author's note: In the book where it is written 'he' or 'him' in reference to the politician, this as much refers to 'her' as in the female politician. It is written on occasion in the masculine, only for simplicity and flow.

Contents

Foreword

Politics is paralysed in Britain and around the world, with democracy struggling to remedy the problems within our country and around the world. Many problems whether they be Brexit, environmental change, war, crime and poverty continue to exist. The short termism within politics and lack of continuity with changing leadership, prevents a united front in resolving the challenges we face.

No single political leaning is wholly to blame, be it left or right. We expect too much from a narrow political clique that lead us, some of whom remain in the same job for decades, sometimes for nearly half a century. What is needed is greater participation and new ideas, more people willing to stand up and be counted, whether to represent their village, constituency or nation. Perform their civic duty.

There has never been a better time to stand up and be counted and seek change in what is becoming a stagnant parliamentary system, one which requires updating and change just like any other sector from time to time, marry the old with the new. We have the best system 'democracy' to serve us, what we need is greater transparency and for democracy to fast forward to the 21st century.

In reading this small book, I hope it drives greater participation in politics here and the rest of the world, whilst encouraging intelligent debate on improving our systems nationally and internationally to make them fit and fair for the modern world.

Background and Introduction

Many theories of governance have come and gone, some good and most bad – historically we have generally started with the worst available governmental systems and evolved to the systems we know today dominated by the democratic capitalist model and on the opposing fence the socialist model, fairer governing systems coming to the fore only as the public awareness has increased and political pressure from the people has been applied over centuries and millennia.

This book is about how we can improve the systems we have from within, to work as they were originally intended. It is not a critique of the Western capitalist system, actually it is an endorsement, it intends however to highlight the defects so that it can work to its full potential. It is an attempt for us the people to get the most out of the system by then removing those inherent defects that the system contains, always has done and continues to do so.

We arrived at our present form of democracy after centuries and millennia of far less democratic forms of governance, absolute rule by kings and barons, feudalism and worse and so why think that what we have now is the best, since up until democracy as we know it today, our ancestors constantly sought to improve the system and increase equality. Why should we not constantly seek to improve our democracy as our ancestors fought to. The truth is the type of system we have is ideal, but the type of people who run it are not, as well as the unwelcome overbearing influence from business interests and lobbyists, and so it needs constant improvement to make our democracy the best it can be.

Key events in the evolution of thinkers, some great and others not, have created new models and evolved existing models of governance. History has shown us examples such as in the Soviet Union or Cambodia, that if left in the hands of any one individual such as a Stalin or Pol Pot it can wreak havoc on a nation and lead to absolute rule and turmoil and in the case of Cambodia genocide, even though the type of governance, socialism should work. If left in the hands of the wrong people in effect nations are doomed. Communism or socialism has gained popularity globally beyond the 20th century only in a handful of countries such as China, North Korea, Venezuela and Vietnam amongst others.

History has shown us that the only system workable on a global scale is the democratic capitalist system we have now and so we must focus our efforts on finding a solution to remove the defects and focus on the positives. Democracy won out against communism and fascism, and so why do we still discuss regressing to alternative governmental models, far left or otherwise that have been shown to be ineffective. Why do we not instead put greater thought into making our present system work better? Since let's be honest, after the fight against communism by the West for more than forty years, no other system will be allowed to dominate the scene and so we have to stick with what we have and make it work better. It's the only way!

The struggle of the Western powers during the Cold War with communism, has led to global capitalism led by the West of the USA, Britain and Western Europe and mirrored around the world being the only workable global model, complete with its trading entities and treaties, it is what essentially binds us today politically and economically. One philosopher Frances Fukuyama went as far as to say that the liberal capitalist model is the best we can have and that 'we have witnessed the end of history,' that democracy had won out with no real competition. But isn't it defeatist to think that we cannot improve on a global model that clearly isn't working around the world and is leading to much inequality and greed? In the midst of all the problems our present system contains today, with corruption, greed and corporate dominance prevalent and a switching off from politics by the public all around the world, isn't that somewhat surrender? How can we say that the system we now have is the best; the evolution of all the previous systems following the struggles of humanity, when the inherent deficiencies are plain for all to see.

If we had witnessed the end of history in terms of the 'perfect political system' then why do we still have all the problems in the world today, why have they not disappeared? Why does war continue unabated against the interests of the people in the country both doing the invading and being invaded? And why do political scandals surface in every country that contains a democracy? Whilst Fukuyama's was a visionary statement, it has been somewhat hijacked by the liberal capitalists as justification for its lack of need for change because supposedly we already have the best workable system, the statement should in theory be 'pending the system working to its full potential' and only then could we have reached that point and the democratic capitalist model be shown to work effectively and for all.

A system that allows outside interests to manipulate and groom career politicians either openly or tacitly and that may lead ultimately to the politician's hands being tied against the interests of his voters, is not the evolution of all the best political models. We have to explore the defects in our system that include breaking the link between power and politics that allows corporate influence to dominate. Further, we need to limit and constrain, or even better remove the extent that policy objectives of the rich and its corporations dominate thinking in politics, or favour war in foreign climes over the interests of the public who have little to gain in any such ventures.

The positive news is that within our present system, we have all the makings of a successful model, but just as in scientific testing, to find the best workable cure we need to identify and acknowledge the defects and inefficiencies and test them to come to a workable solution. This book is not a critique of business or corporations, since business and trade is good for us all, and everyone should be better off over time through increased competition. When that crosses over into politics and leads to decision making in favour of corporate profits against the good of the people that is no longer a good thing and people suffer. We need to even the balance in favour of the public.

As will be explained, the great problems our political system possesses, is the dominance of career seeking politicians who often favour their corporate backers over the electorate in order to remain in their job over the long term. Added to that is the embedding of corporate power within politics through lobbying, campaign funding and revolving door politics, where politicians go into the private sector and back into politics in their own interest and make decisions in favour of their previous or future employers. The positive news is the link can be broken and politics can be free of outside influence, but steps have to be taken. This book will go on to explain the background to the problem and the steps we need to take to cleanse our system to allow it to work as it should.

For the next chapter we will look at the character fit of those who end up in the positions of power and identify that whilst those motivations might satisfy the aspiring politician's desires, they are on the contrary detrimental to the public at large.

CHAPTER 1

Career politicians and the mirage of choice

We are given the mirage of choice, able to vote only on candidates available to us carefully selected by a given party, but is there really a choice when we can vote on only those candidates themselves who choose to be there, not candidates recruited from wider society that didn't have a predetermined interest to enter politics? Wouldn't someone of that ilk, not egotistically driven or obsessively determined to dominate in politics be better suited to serve us more honestly and openly, than someone who entered politics with no real experience of the outside world and who is seeking a career, rather than only representing the public. We often see politicians, particularly those aiming for the top positions bent on power and control to achieve their personal desires be it for ego, lust for power or greatness, all character traits that we regularly see in politicians except perhaps not the word 'greatness'. Wouldn't real choice imply that everyone should be a possible candidate, not only those career politicians that at present make up the majority of the available pool of candidates from which we can presently vote upon.

We don't choose our politicians, we choose amongst an available pool of candidates carefully selected from the left and right spectrum of politics, generally by Labour, the Conservatives and the Lib Dems in the UK or the Democrats and Republicans in the USA. And thus we vote on a pool of candidates that decided to enter politics often for self-interest. We inevitably end up with the problem of having a greater pool of politicians of that mind-set that ultimately dominate politics and all too often rise to the top positions. We end up with a pool of career politicians that entered politics often for egotistical reasons, with an inflated ego and drive for power, fame and success, believing perhaps that they are better than the rest of us, and uniquely able to perform the role.

It is possible that the wrong motivations inspire many politicians towards seeking a career in politics. The idea and expectation of attention and fame may inspire a career in politics that puts one in the position of power and greater desirability, as well as the potential to change the direction of ones country or the world, and options for a comfortable retirement and top connections. But are those motivations the character traits of someone who we want representing us? Absolutely not. Change is sometimes needed for the country and the world to move on and progress, but the character profile of the career politician shouldn't be the person to lead it, but we let them.

The career politician will develop a skill for deal making and public speaking, something that most of us could acquire over time if we entered political office. Since those skills are not unique to the politician, just skills of which the more successful who have risen to the top have in greater abundance than other politicians. The politician will develop skills over time, but then so would anybody else capable and willing and he will eventually climb the political ladders of progress, and by a deft hand, being more accomplished than the rest of the pool of career politicians at speaking, deal making and timing and no doubt being in favour to his superiors at that time, eventually be welcomed to the higher echelons of government and cabinet office.

Regardless in this instance, if we vote left or right, socialist or any other we don't have the best available candidates in our midst, we have only the choice of those politicians that decided to enter this most important of all trades that represent us the world over. We have the mirage of choice but that choice is largely limited to those career politicians that entered the political fray as opposed to other individuals such as the banker, the doctor, lawyer or others that chose another type of employment. Perhaps someone of another character profile would undoubtedly serve us better.

In the early life of the career politician no doubt many have motivations to improve the public good, but that motivation isn't exceptional, in other trades we all seek to do that in some way. No doubt the possibility of fame and greatness motivated many an individual to enter politics. He daydreams of himself being on TV, received by a great audience and a rapturous applause, in a public square standing on a soapbox clapped by a vast audience, eventually promoted to hold the trappings of a great office of state, perhaps even the prime minister. The motivations of the career building politician aren't ideal character traits to serve well in the position over time; these motivations benefitting more the individual entering politics, their career and ambitions, not necessarily their constituents or the nation. And yet how are they any better suited to the role than others from amongst the rest of society.

Any number of reasons can propel someone to seek a career straight out of school or university, or only a few years work in the real world into politics, and some may be noble and justified. But on the whole when we have only career politicians who make up the bulk of those who represent us and when the pool of career politicians is dominated by those of a similar mind-set and motivation, we inevitably end up with a system ripe for greed, self-serving and corruption. For what is good for him and his desires, is that someone who is likely to represent the public well? In a pool of career politicians, many of the same mould, where are the outstanding candidates amongst them? Well they probably chose other more lucrative careers, unfortunately starving the nation of better talent who could represent us better. Does the character profile of a career politician seem like an ideal candidate as a member of parliament, a cabinet minister, a senator or congressman, or even a prime minister or president... absolutely not, yet it happens often.

Where we have a system that allows for the establishment of career politicians, that perhaps don't have their voters interests at heart and who may stay in that role for life with their parties' backing, shouldn't we look at a system whereby that wasn't a given, one where not just by choosing to enter politics one becomes a politician, but perhaps a system whereby there is no certainty and guaranteed longevity in politics for the career politician. One where there is a wider pool of people entering politics from which to choose.

What alternative system and safeguards could we look at to develop a greater pool of honest and selfless candidates to enter politics, that are there not just because they chose that office, but people from a broader spectrum of the country, who perhaps may not have thought to enter politics in the first place.

Throughout the world there is one constant and certainty; corruption is endemic and prevalent in politics all around the world and democracy is no exception to that rule, let alone other less democratic systems either communistic or dictatorial, no country is immune. Whichever side the politician sits on the fence, whether on the left, right or centre, often the same outcome results; favouritism, bribery, corruption and corporate influence in politics prevails against the public will and thus a malfunctioning democratic capitalism system. Before going into detail about what can be done to counter this problem, let's first have a look at how this recurring problem happens in the first place.

We look at politicians whether we like them or not, often sometimes in awe, as figures of importance separate from the rest of us, we see them on TV or in the newspapers and attach a special importance to them, that perhaps they've done something extraordinary to reach that position when in fact that may not be true. It's akin to how people in Victorian and Edwardian times looked up to the aristocracy with their titles, gowns and mansions as the celebrities of the day, people to look up to and respect without question. The prevalence of politicians and those in the House of Lords nowadays isn't much different, more so politicians are on the news or in the papers, there are grand titles and we look up to them to represent and lead us well. The importance of the political world is thrust upon us via the air time it receives on the TV news and in the newspapers so judging by its prevalence in our daily lives, its impact on jobs and income, shouldn't we all participate more proactively ourselves considering how politics affects us all? Little do we know that perhaps many of us if we chose to enter that career path could contribute and achieve political success. Many of us complain about politicians and the state of our country, and of the world, but we don't offer to get involved. Just leaving the politicians to manage the nations politics themselves. We shouldn't be surprised that they mess it up, because self interest takes over, and the public switch off since we don't have the best talent representing us in the first place. We vote but nothing really changes, yet we are also responsible for the status quo since we complain about the system, corruption and incompetence but we aren't willing to participate or provide a real solution.

This homage to the politician just like to the aristocracy and royals in years gone by is unnecessary since they have done nothing special except entering the world of politics along with hard work no doubt, when others didn't – they entered and you didn't, just that – it's that simple. And thus a pool of politicians has emerged that dominates the capitalist systems of the world, dominated and run by individuals driven and sometimes bent on personal ambition and career growth, not necessarily working for the greater good of the public. This career entry is juxtaposed to the character less egotistical and not bent only on political ambition that chose another career, the character that represents the majority of the public, who isn't interested in a career in politics and thus only watches the politician on TV often detached from their world, and surmising that they may perhaps be uniquely able and suitable, because they meet with other globally important people from time to time and make important decisions nationally and globally that affect us all. Ultimately we are thus left with a pool of politicians dominated by people of the wrong psyche to represent us, and not in our best interests.

It is not to say that all politicians are self-interested or self-serving, there are decent motivated and hardworking politicians inspired by causes which matter deeply to them and their voters, causes for which they fight for all their political life, often avoiding high office as a result because they are not able to be moulded, bribed or cajoled to follow the system in pursuit of personal ambition, wealth and title. Often these politicians are admired and respected by both sides of the chamber, across the left and right spectrum of politics precisely because they stick to their beliefs and causes, rather than pursuing personal ambition and promotion, perhaps achievable should they conform to the career politician mould.

Look at it like this, three friends from university go into separate careers, one becomes a banker and does very well for himself, the other becomes a doctor and also excels and builds a practice and the third friend decides that he shall have a career in politics. In real life this would be millions of people going about their jobs. A lot is still to be done by the politician, to climb the career ladder of the political world, but the inevitability of a finite pool of characters entering politics in the first place, leads to the inevitability of him eventually becoming an MP or senator or perhaps high office eventually with hard work and focus, and should he have his marbles, a deft hand for negotiating, ability to forge the right contacts to help his career progression and be able to speak well in public.

In fact all three friends, being high achievers within their chosen professions, will go far and in terms of income, the banker will earn millions, the doctor earns a couple of hundred thousand pounds plus and the rising politician much less on perhaps seventy to eighty thousand pounds a year. All three succeed in their careers and our politician friend will eventually rise to a cabinet post and perhaps even prime minister or president depending where he is, earning a good deal more, but still not nearly as much as his friends in other careers. In terms of income, he isn't the greatest of successes, but in terms of public appearances, prevalence in the media; on TV and in the newspapers, his image as a finely tuned public speaker after years or perhaps decades of practice would to the average Joe put our politician friend in the perceived position to the public at least, of a great success and achiever. These are often the motivations of our career politicians. With all the trappings of power, living in Downing Street, the White House or a presidential palace, the armoured motorcade, ministerial car, association only with other statesmen of the world, at least that's the perspective our media portrays to us; the state banquets and deciding on our future as a nation make this person or any persons involved in the decision making with the cabinet very important, and appear as a great success amongst all career options. Naturally the senior politician will retire well and have the option to make far more than their career salary through speaking engagements and advisory posts afterwards. Advising businesses and other countries on the unique knowledge they gained throughout their career in politics.

By looking at this figure of success, or the perception of this career holding all the trappings of success, we can perhaps delve into some of the motives of why someone would be attracted to that position of power in the first place, despite it not offering either the greatest financial rewards compared to the two university friends, the banker and the doctor, let alone the privacy implications and inevitable background checks that any aspiring politician would be subjected to against their will. Increasingly pervasive in the social media age as well as the unstable nature of the job such as losing an election.

The problem we face is that by the law of numbers and the inevitability that someone has to fill a position in government or the party, be it on the left or right, the politician who is given a free hand to enter politics in a presently finite pool, multiplied in factor by hundreds of thousands around the world gives us a pool of career driven, single minded politicians that on the whole dominate politics worldwide, this most important of sectors to serve the public good, with many serving their own interests as opposed to the public good. We have our career politician, safe in his seat not because he is the best man for the job, but because he went for that job and others didn't, those two other friends became a banker and a doctor, but seen on the global level this would be hundreds of millions of people going about their careers that chose another job instead of politics. Granted he may have worked hard to get there, but all of us can claim to work hard in our given trade, that is not a trait unique to the career politician.

Although some politicians really are very devoted and driven to serve the public honestly and fairly, they don't represent the majority. Perhaps less than 20% can claim to do so in reality, and on the whole, for that 80%, what makes them better and more capable than the rest of us to serve office in politics? Nothing, except the fact that they entered politics and the rest of us didn't, and entered other trades. The simplification is simply to drum home the point that not necessarily the best and brightest enter the world of politics. Over time, as he fine tunes his style and becomes a decent public speaker, the politician may become impressive and represent us well, or at least appear to do so. Some top politicians are impressive speakers, artists at persuasion and public speaking with carefully choreographed hand moves, able to gesticulate better than any puppet to express a point. He would be an example of someone destined for high office under our present system, where the TV friendly and convincing politician is generally the one who dominates and gets ahead.

Since politicians such as the influential speaker are usually destined to lead us, does that mean that he or she is the best person for the job, or even has the policies best suited to the country? Not necessarily, since the character fit of an influential or charismatic politician often is placed or thrust into power precisely because they are convincing and are thus backed by big business as their man, able to convince the public or parliament, truthfully or untruthfully, to accept unpopular actions such as war or other unpopular policies and not necessarily the best man for the job, or most able to serve the public good. Perhaps a less inspiring, less charismatic politician would better serve the role, but he or she is unlikely to convince the electorate or the media and by being less career driven would be less likely to betray on their ideals and do favours for either lobbyists or campaign donors.

If the desire for power for its own sake as well as glory and success is the main draw for someone seeking high office, then shouldn't we do something about creating a system whereby a greater pool of people enter the political trade and not only those attracted to politics for the wrong motivations, that benefit the career politician over the public? Due to its great importance of representing the nation and the world ultimately, shouldn't we seek out the very best, brightest and honest from our citizenry and allow them to become involved in this most important of careers, as opposed to drawing from a pool of potential politicians, being only those who decided to enter politics, which inevitability results in us being led by people that favour their career and the trappings of power, over the good of the nation.

Over time, the politician becomes absorbed into the political world and detached from the people he was elected to represent, drawn into the 'political bubble' within politics that makes our politicians often detached from us and beholden to the influence and hype that arises from the political centre of any country be it the Westminster or Capitol Hill bubble.

Perhaps we don't have the best people involved in politics because the salary isn't a big enough draw for the best and brightest, that instead choose other careers. Perhaps the salary should be higher to attract better talent? We end up with a bulk of average candidates becoming politicians on fairly good salaries but with the very successful knowing full well later on that they can earn far more at retirement. Not only that, but when we see very rich politicians, now multi millionaires commanding hundreds of thousands of dollars or pounds from individual speeches, often in an advisory capacity to big business, imparting their unique insider knowledge to the corporate world, we find our leading politicians more fine-tuned to serve the interests of business. We have to ask the question, which side are they serving? The business community or the people they were elected to represent?

When we look at the career driven politicians of the Western world that put more effort into campaign funding than serving their electorate, more interested in re-election than serving the people under their present term of office, and the corrupt politicians or dictators across the world, the same corruption prevails, they have sold on their added value of giving to humanity by serving in order to achieve personal gain. And herein we have the catch 22 in politics, that in order to get ahead in politics and to be a big player and rise up through the ranks of the party, the politician must inevitably betray on their original ideals and decent intentions to get ahead and up the career ladder. Since the political environment in many countries may prevent progress if one doesn't accept bribes or favours in some form.

The politician may now be perhaps ten or twenty years into their political career, a large house, several cars, and maybe costly school fees enter the fray and the comfort of a post political job is all the more important, and so the politician will often lay the foundations for a post political job in a large corporation that seeks insider knowledge of working government to further their corporate influence and profits. The politician seeks a favourable retirement; a general may wish to feather his nest and build a comfortable life for retirement and thus impart his knowledge on military contractors with whom he would've liaised with in his senior defence role, he may now find himself very employable to defence contractors who would gladly employ someone with such immense and unique insider knowledge of the running of government defence policy, to aid them in their business ventures. This is no critique of those corporations, that only seek a competitive advantage, since it is the government that encourages and allows the revolving doors between the corporate and political world to happen. The buck and responsibility lies with the government and the political world and what they permit as acceptable.

What we have now is someone in a role originally to serve the public, but now is out to serve himself, on a global scale across the world we see the same pattern and problems. For the politician out of the three friends, which on a global level would be hundreds of thousands of people across all nations attracted to the trappings of political office, entering the political world in many instances due to serve a life as a career politician against the greater good of the public. Our politician friend chose that career along with his colleagues across the world and we thus have a majority pool of politicians that we would absolutely not want representing us, that are being allowed to do so because the door is open to only those who seek office to be given the green light to represent us. The career politician in one nation is magnified and mirrored around the world and thus the electorate everywhere complains about the standard and state of their country's politicians and general politics. No country is immune, we all face the same problems and challenges. The positive news is that the solution that works for one nation, would work for all nations and politics can be cleaned up globally by changing the nature of those who enter or work in politics, nation by nation until globally we have a much improved system.

CHAPTER 2

Introducing 'Jury Service style' politics and limiting political careers to ten years

No matter what political system we have in the world, under the present arrangements, corruption, greed and an oversupply of egotistically self-serving politicians prevails and are allowed to dominate the world of politics. We allow those with a predetermined interest in politics to dominate, when perhaps a broader spread from society, with a career behind them, would be better suited to serve us. Politics is doomed to involve corruption and backhanders, unless we prevent the career politicians from having the choice to enter and remain in politics indefinitely, under their terms. We must limit the political term and open up entry into politics to us all.

The only solution is to move to a 'jury service style' of politics where everyone is expected during their lifetime between the ages of twenty-one and sixty to participate in the political world in some way shape or form. Much like any member of the UK public is obligated to serve on a jury once in their lifetime if asked. Initially we hope more people will run to be an MP which would widen the pool of candidates from which to choose. Candidates would serve five-year terms as an MP as they do presently and after five years may seek re-election with their constituency or apply for a cabinet role. They will be expected to sign an agreement to avoid conflicts of interest, that they will not enter related employment following their five or ten-year stint.

Every year posts will be nationally advertised for which the public would be required to assist at least once in their lifetime between the ages of twenty-one and sixty. The options range from one year to five years for unelected and elected positions, from junior posts to political office and the relevant role would seek to match the candidates skill set. So someone presently working in a health related role could work in the health department, more people across sectors working within an equivalent department bringing relevant up-to-date knowledge to the department and policy areas. The more aspiring may seek elected office whereas others may prefer to have a quiet background role but nonetheless within the political sphere and thus performing their civic duty. Internationally, some systems will have a different process but the theory if acted upon can improve politics universally.

It is hoped that people would willingly want to participate and that it wouldn't be a burden to be involved, since we are all as one looking to tidy up politics and participate in something that affects us all in some way or another. Candidates would have the option to defer their political service were the time not right, but would be expected at some time to contribute. In many cases, roles could be fast tracked for the unemployed so that they could use their existing experience in a role and become further skilled during one to five years' service, increasing their skill set and making themselves more attractive job wise after their political service. It is a 'win win' scenario, both to the individual and to the country, and many people of all ages either in or out of employment would, it's hoped, be glad to serve their country in some capacity, bringing some of their skill set to a role. The idea is to draw upon a diverse populace to serve the public willingly, not to punish the successful that unwillingly are required to serve the public. For that reason there would be opt outs or deferments for people with no desire or interest to serve or who are absolutely opposed to political service. Nobody can then say that they haven't had a chance to be involved in politics, or had the chance to clean up politics since we would have either all been directly involved somehow in our lifetime, or at least had the option.

By creating this form of 'jury service' to the world of politics what can we expect to see? Firstly we will have a larger pool from which to choose our politicians across the whole country that could serve in government. We have a variety of core sectors in any country that runs services essential to the effective running of that country. The individual will be expected to bring some real world experience into the world of politics and should they run for MP or a cabinet post, have some specific background experience to make them relevant and attractive to voters.

By limiting the term any politician can serve we are doing a few things. Significantly reducing the ability for a politician to gain contacts and be groomed over a generation by those businesses that seek to influence and manipulate politicians for gain and favour. We seek to break this link between corruption and favouritism which is allowed to happen, such as the seeking of campaign donations, the lobbyist or corporation seeking influence and greater profits at the expense of impartiality and fairness. In so doing by limiting time served, there is less opportunity for politicians to be groomed in return for favours, since the political life of the politician is limited to ten years, with many expected to serve five-year terms.

One can envisage a system whereby professionals from the health service, perhaps a former GP would make a fine addition to the health sector, whether as an adviser, an elected MP or any role within the functioning government or department related to their skill set and background. Whatever the level of experience and seniority, everyone matters and the whole and not the individual, is the key to success. Eventually this MP may become the health secretary, bringing their unique perspective to the role. We would be bringing competition into the whole world of politics, and ending the permanent staffer and the career politician as well as selected appointees to key political positions. Imagine what sort of benefit and unique perspectives a former surgeon, doctor or nurse could bring to the health department through first-hand experience. These potential examples of genuine public servants, some of whom work long hours for little pay could offer genuine selfless service to government. How much more useful would the input be, from someone recruited from this sector, than an MP who once in a while cuts a ribbon to open a new hospital, but has never worked in the sector, has no real knowledge except through advisers and briefing notes, and hasn't worked half as hard as the people in that sector to know the real challenges. Instead entering politics straight from university or perhaps after working only a few years.

The professional career politician is unlikely to offer any more value to an office of state than to someone with real world experience, with a vision and ideas to improve any given sector. The added competition at a general election would excite the public and probably put the career politician health secretary out of work, as he struggles to argue his case for being a better candidate than the former GP or surgeon to run the health sector. Neither is there any real benefit to us of our ministers of state, advisors and civil service staff serving particularly long periods in office. After all, secretaries of state for any department may be waiting to be promoted to what they deem a better and more senior role such as home secretary, foreign secretary or eventually prime minister viewing the health, transport or environment department only as a stepping stone. But to our new breed of MPs, with more real world experience as well as a genuine will to serve, and able to bring their unique skills to the role, that would be much less likely to happen, since they will serve and represent that role of which they have a unique perspective on and for which they were elected. They would likely stay in the role for the duration rather than career hop into more senior roles, since they would likely be elected because of their unique perspective and knowledge that they could bring to the post that they were elected to. How often do we see a government minister such as a health secretary, or an education secretary serving one or two years, sometimes only months, before moving department either due to a cabinet reshuffle, or because they sought a more senior role in their perceived estimation? What prior experience can a cabinet minister bring to a role without serving in that sector previously, apart from an ability to learn quickly that most of us could also claim to do? What benefit is there in having MPs and cabinet ministers representing positions of which they have no previous knowledge or real world experience, perhaps only viewing the role as a stepping stone to greater success later on?

The prospect of serving within a senior cabinet role is often the motivation and driver for the career politician. These are the roles that have all the trappings of success; the large salary, ministerial car, lucrative future job prospects, making decisions amongst other international statesmen and afterwards a comfortable retirement. Wouldn't it be better if these roles had greater competition and a maximum limit of a ten-year political term? We would have greater synergy, focus and success within the relevant departments than now, if the people who ran and made decisions in those departments had more real world experience.

To summarise, we are seeking a wider pool of candidates from across broader society to serve across the left and right of politics, as MPs and within the wider world of government and politics.

CHAPTER 3

Ending revolving door politics

The problem of the revolving door in politics is at every level and the reason for much distrust as former politicians across departments such as defence, treasury, food and pharmaceuticals often go and work for those same companies afterwards in well paid advisory or directorship roles, that were vying for contracts with them and their departments, when they were in government. A gross conflict of interest but which is often overlooked and is widespread, particularly in the USA. At what point may the public benefit from this system of revolving door appointments inside and outside of politics? This type of career politician, serves first his campaign backers and second the public once his funding is assured. One only needs to look at who funds the political parties to know whose interests are truly being served. Why would a campaign backer financially support both republican and democratic candidates if not to influence those politicians directly, since the policies of the two parties are far apart? The big corporations of defence, pharmaceuticals and Wall Street are allowed to have undue influence in politics precisely because of the presence of campaign funding and of the revolving doors in politics. It ensures the corporate interest is served over that of the public, over the lifetime of the career politician.

Why has this been allowed to happen? It's because the wrong character profile from a reduced pool of available candidates has been allowed to dominate politics in the first place, thus allowing the career politician through lack of better competition to be able to get ahead. But crucially the second reason is because over time due to serving a long career in politics, he is able to feather his own nest through the constant need to seek campaign funds and the regular contact with lobby groups. He is obliged to support their interests over the people he should really be serving, providing favours for those campaign donors who helped him get elected in the first place.

The opportunity for our career politicians to serve twenty or thirty years in office and to be influenced over the course of their political life, as well as seek post-political careers whilst in office before political retirement should end. The revolving door from the political world and the corporate world should be shut. However, unfortunately many politicians enter into the revolving doors of politics and work for corporations on which they have inside knowledge, by preventing this conflict of interest and ensuring that politicians will not enter into employment following their term of office in conflict with their political role, this can only benefit the public and country at large.

In the economic crash of 2008, there were senior staff working in the US treasury involved in bailing out their former employers, deciding which banks survived and which fell by the wayside. Examples of bias and conflicts of interest such as this shouldn't be permitted under a healthy working system.

A potential financial scandal was soon overlooked because the bailout worked, but the favouritism and lack of impartiality on which banks would survive and which wouldn't, should not have involved decision makers with a conflict of interest. Since it was legal and had the appearance of legitimacy it was soon forgotten about since the crisis was allayed, but the impossible to pay back debt to the public remained and further eroded public trust. Wherever there are profits to be made and influence bought, politicians will slip into and out of the corporate sector as and when it suits them or should they face unexpected electoral defeat.

The problems of corruption and favouritism through pre-existing links with corporations and lobbyists are something that taints our democracies across the world and is not isolated to any one country or continent, it is global. It happens and will continue to happen unless we prevent the wrong type of politician from being able to obtain power and remain there as a career politician indefinitely, until we close the revolving doors between the corporate world and politics and remove corporate involvement in campaign financing.

Surely a transparent government would enact laws preventing the moving into and out of the corporate sector from a related political post, but instead we regularly see senators or congressmen openly supporting the companies or organisations that financially backed their campaign. The problems are systemic and can only be removed by changing the type of people entering politics, reducing their time served and ending the revolving doors between politics and the corporate world. Those politicians over a period of twenty, thirty or perhaps forty-year careers have feathered their nests and made their contacts, corruption becomes embedded and those campaign donors will be there for life as long as the politician doesn't make an about turn. Because surely at that point if his views change, the funding will stop and the opportunity of a career outside of politics would disappear. The financial backer will find another mouldable candidate to support, a most unattractive outcome to the career politician who seeks stability and re-election above all else.

Corporations and lobbyists generally only support politicians to receive favour; corporate influence is not there for the benefit of the public at large, the campaign donations and promises of a job through the revolving doors of the political and corporate world are all part of the package. This isn't beneficial to the public, and the link should be broken. But it can only be broken if the political term of a politician is capped at ten years. A dishonest politician would be unlikely to serve beyond a five-year term, and unable to serve beyond ten years. This greatly reduces there being sufficient time to seek and do favours due to the limited term of office, and by signing a 'no conflicts of interest agreement' that he shall not enter the employment of any company that he has entered into partnership with whilst in government, the revolving doors of the political and corporate world would be shut for good.

A greater influx of politicians over a range of core government departments such as the health, defence, home and foreign office has been seen here to be possible. A more competitive and open politics would be advantageous in numerous ways, from having experts and professionals from outside of politics working within those government departments, doctors and nurses in the health department, and former vice chancellors and head teachers in the education department. By there being a maximum term of ten years, we thus break the corruption and favouritism that sucks the productive value out of our nations and stunts economic growth, leaving us in an endless distrust of our politicians to the extent that many do not see the benefit in voting for any party at all. A public totally cut off from politics, but yet their life being very much interwoven with the decisions of those politicians.

Could someone more noble and respected of the public carry out a prime ministerial or presidential role more effectively, more impartial and closer to the public sentiment than what we have seen in the last ten or twenty years or the generation before that? Avoiding unnecessary wars and gross overspending as well as financial mis-management, why certainly! Without career politicians making decisions in sectors that they have no history of working in, nor being beholden to pressure groups, big corporations, big defence contractors and hawkish generals, we certainly could pursue a different path for our country and humanity in the process, leading by example and becoming a beacon to the world.

With the public further involved in the selection process and there not being the opportunity for politicians to be groomed by lobbyists and corporate donors throughout long careers, we can remove the hawkish leader, driven in his belief system by a one sided view of the world. A system of removing the career politician, selecting from a wider pool of candidates as well as limiting terms to ten years, with the public getting the final say on the top governmental positions, is the only way to create stable government and enable our present system to work efficiently in the interests of the public, whilst being free of corruption and bribes.

This is why not only do we have to remove the career politician from politics but also the permanent lobbyists and advisers who represent outside interests and big business. When we allow a system of revolving doors between corporate chiefs and the upper echelons of government, we are opening the system up to abuse, greed and corruption, it is inevitable that favours and backhanders will be given. No one should be surprised about this under the present system, frustrated yes but not surprised, because the system as it is allows it to happen.

In the case of the education sector, wouldn't it be better to let primary and secondary school head teachers and former university vice chancellors get together and work on education policy, perhaps chosen from amongst candidates shortly into an early retirement they may be glad to get out of? Some would gladly serve and could bring real value, especially if their input could benefit their schools, district and country directly. Wouldn't it be more favourable to have a former head of the railways, or a land planner work in the transport or housing departments respectively, and represent a cabinet seat equivalent to their working background, rather than someone with little or no experience? Surely the accumulated experience over years in their professional capacity offers more to the public good than the young cabinet minister, who usually enters politics shortly after university, with little or no real life experience and who may view a perceived 'minor' junior ministerial seat only as a springboard for a more senior position later on.

The world surrounding politics needs to be opened up to the general public from between one to five-year roles to enable transparency and a greater inclusivity on our part. No longer can we then say that politicians are a waste of time or don't know what they're doing, since we all would have had an opportunity to be involved in either a minor or senior capacity in the world of politics, from between one to five years between the ages of twenty-one to sixty. Added to that is the option of running for MP for between five to ten years in elected office.

CHAPTER 4

Avoiding seesaw party politics and more MPs with real world experience

Since the ideal for a nation is continuing and stable core departments of the country, it's more imperative that we have greater consistency in government and fewer swings between the left and right over time. There is little benefit in the additional costs to the taxpayer and wasted billions through policies enacted and then simply cancelled over the term of the following government.

An MP seeking re-election after five years should have excelled if they are to be re-elected, not merely put their name forward for a safe seat, and the public should be able to see clearly what they have achieved and why they continue to wish to serve in government. Whilst governments may have separate agendas in selecting candidates for cabinet roles due to seniority and promotions within government, in this case, by more MPs and cabinet ministers involved in government with real world experience and with greater transparency within their respective departments, we allow for greater continuity and success within government departments, as common sense decision making replaces party politics.

Often, we see one administration proposing a piece of legislation such as a large spending project or deregulation, with the opposition party threatening a reversal of policies at the next election. With a more honest and open government we could avoid these costly ideological swings in government projects between the left and right, that in the long term cost the country dearly. Too often we see policies enacted under one government then simply cancelled under the next, or at threat of being – creating disorder, uncertainty and great cost to the taxpayer.

We can see history repeating itself as the nation shifts to the right after a long Labour government or to the left after a long Conservative government. After several years of a Labour government during the late nineties and two thousands and closer EU integration, vast government overspends, unpopular wars and government largesse, the country shifted right as the Conservative government set out to reverse policy and run a tighter ship on the economy. The shift to the right over that time and the consequent distancing from EU policy and rules, in contrast to Labour policy, has ultimately led to Brexit. Inevitably, at some point after the next Conservative government, Labour will seek to unwind and reverse Conservative policy. Over time, we see too much stopping and starting of projects as one government goes and another arrives. The nations crime levels and the NHS become a political football, when really, management and oversight should be with a long term outlook with cross party focus, in order to form a consistent plan that won't simply be scrapped later, decisions separated from party political objectives. No single party is right or wrong, simply going with the public mood at the time and their party policy, but the stop start politics, opening and cancelling of large public works projects in the end costs the public dearly in wasted taxpayer spending. Not to mention delays or cuts across government departments such as the NHS, Social Security or Home Office that affect us all directly.

There is often little continuity or stability in policy and thus no long terms gains for the country in these inevitable radical shifts between the left and right. Wouldn't a system accepting these generally given truths be more effective if it was able to work to prevent those big shifts between the left and right and vice versa, with more continuity and permanence where policy ideas were similar? Wouldn't it be more practical and helpful for the country's better governance? Wouldn't more parliamentarians with real world experience, and chosen by the public to key cabinet posts, be more preferable than ministerial seats dished out behind closed doors?

An MP or Senator that served in the police force may be elected to run the Home Office or their respective department, given their background, in this case the candidate having an expert knowledge and track record of reducing crime. Many would gladly run for a role and offer valuable real life experience to a position. The likelihood is that a Home Secretary with previous experience in the police force would be a better match with her accumulated knowledge than our recently promoted cabinet minister who only days before might have been serving as Education or Transport Minister, something totally unrelated. Thrust into the position with droves of papers and without much knowledge of the office at hand, and in effect likely prey to the opinion and will of advisors and speechwriters, who themselves may have links and vested interests with lobbying groups. Perhaps holding great influence despite not being elected themselves; in this instance the unelected staff member may hold great sway over the elected member in their advisory role. The problem is not limited to career politicians but also career civil servants and all those grey areas where business can have undue influence over the political domain. That is why broader public involvement is needed across the world at all levels of government and politics with roles capped at ten years.

Over the UK, the USA and across the world the same truth applies; corporate influence, corruption and favouritism is embedded in politics, whether on a small or large scale and is unavoidable without changes within the system. Perhaps in

Western democracies corruption is more subtle, such as the expenses scandal in the UK of 2009 which shamed many politicians into retirement. In the USA the problem is more serious since senators and congressmen rely on corporate backers in order to even run as a candidate, and so politicians are susceptible to corporate interference, blackmail and bribery, pretty much from the outset of their careers.

CHAPTER 5

Greater public involvement in candidate selection

The political parties such as the Conservatives, Labour or Liberal Democrats select a candidate to represent a constituency. Across the UK as of 2020 there were 650 constituencies with an MP elected to represent the people of that constituency. Usually when starting out, a twenty or thirty something aspiring politician will fight an unwinnable seat in either a council or parliamentary role. The politician would have been selected by the party committee for the constituency to run, and only when he runs for elected office will the public have had a first glimpse of the candidate. Here the politician will do the groundwork and lay the foundations for since he is unlikely to win, later on he shall be given a more winnable seat by the party, having proven himself. This reflects the present situation in the UK of how one enters politics.

As a young aspiring MP fights an unwinnable seat in order to get their name out and be rewarded with a more winnable seat later on by the party machinery of Labour or the Conservatives. Even former Prime Ministers David Cameron, Margaret Thatcher and Tony Blair would have gone through this trial before becoming established politicians.

How about greater public involvement in candidate selection and greater transparency? Now the public would vote on who fills those junior or senior cabinet roles and will have more involvement in the direction of their country from the bottom up, the decision making not controlled only by those parties themselves.

The present arrangement of political parties deciding who runs to represent a seat and who doesn't should be updated, and the public should be given greater involvement and transparency in candidate selection. Not the present situation of the party selecting the candidate who is then guaranteed election and then re-election in perpetuity for perhaps thirty, forty or fifty years once in a safe seat. Since this would be the same for all parties there should be no party favouritism any more. In this instance we can vote for the candidate of our choice, not just for the Labour or Conservative candidate pre-selected by the party. This would remove the often-seen parachuted politician who is fast-tracked into government into a very winnable seat but who is often without any background to the area or the constituents of whom he is seeking votes.

In its place within any given constituency, for any given party leaning, a shortlist of five candidates can be drawn up for which the public votes upon. Campaign funding should be the same for all candidates and parties and no private funding should be permitted. The same benefits could be seen in the USA. If there is a shortlist of at least five candidates to run for either the democrats and the republicans, with the public voting on the candidates to run as well as the party, that not being left to the party to decide, in effect we are creating an additional election, for us to choose on the candidate to represent us.

In the UK, the general election would follow later with the winning candidate representing that constituency. We are trying to remove ideology and party politics from decision making and move towards common sense politics, politicians that appeal to the public at large, not just party appointees. The deciding of which candidates to represent any given party should not be left alone for the party machinery to decide upon.

The aim of a more inclusive and open political climate is not to thrust people into positions for which they do not want to serve, but to widen the pool from which to choose those who represent us at a general election. Anybody driven by a passion for public service may run for elected office as candidates. The public will be able to make their own judgements as to the more desirable candidate, based on the already greater available choice. Added to that, the public will be able to differentiate between the existing career politicians and the new breed, and make their own judgements. After all there are many good MPs, cabinet ministers and councillors out there on the left and right of politics and they should be allowed to pursue politics with free will, some who have selflessly fought their campaigns and maintained consistent beliefs in the public interest over their career. It would not be prudent to exclude them from a genuine wish to serve the public but it's still necessary to curb a career to ten years, to reduce corruption, and maintain consistency and fairness.

With a transparent candidate selection process by the parties several months before a general election, the public can select who they really want to represent them, not someone selected based on party loyalties. The candidate will represent his or her constituency for five years and be able to seek re-election up to a maximum term of ten years. To aid in transition, all existing politicians would be able to serve another ten years, no sudden retirements are necessary. The public will be more involved than ever with greater transparency and a wider choice of candidates involved.

CHAPTER 6

Better decision making between the parties and greater national stability

Under this arrangement we maintain our elections for constituency seats except that we have widened the available talent for those that enter politics and also at the same time involved the public in the selection of party candidates, something originally decided privately by the party. How then, could we approach governing on a national scale in relation to ministerial positions?

Wouldn't time, money and stress be saved by both the government and the public if some power is shared more often and decisions taken into account with a longer-term focus? How about the serving cabinet minister and shadow cabinet minister working closer together and perhaps better still, with real world experience in the department for which they work? Less party politics and more practical benefit to the public. More cabinet posts held by MPs with skills and a working background in relation to their cabinet seat and thus being able to bring real world experience and insight to their role.

If Labour had won the last general election, renationalisation was a major policy objective of Corbyn's Labour Party and the public taxpayer would have to again subsidise the costs to bring about the renationalisation. What though, is the guarantee in our present state of politics that if enacted under a Labour government, the Conservatives don't privatise the railways again in fifteen or twenty years' time, reversing the decision which would lead to more upheaval, costs and delays. Better to have some permanence and long term decision making between the parties now. Work together and share in decision making to get the best possible long term outcome for the country.

We have delegated our national wellbeing and decision making over vital services that affect us all and that we need and use on a regular basis such as defence, the NHS, police, schools, railways and buses largely to those self-motivated career politicians in charge of departments that they often ruin through incompetence, mismanagement or short sighted and ill thought out polices. Aren't we ultimately responsible for not having widened the pool of candidates to represent us? And instead create a system whereby experienced hands run relevant departments according to their background knowledge and skill set of which they have unique knowledge that they can bring to the role; retired GP's and doctors to the health department, business leaders and entrepreneurs offering input into government business departments and the treasury.

By removing one influential party that won a large portion of the public vote from any decision making and largely keeping them in the dark about government policy, it effectively encourages future instability. In the future we may have regular hung parliaments, and no majority government. Better to pre-empt the stalemate and improve cross party politics now. Better to find a common ground than to engage in stop start policies that end up costly and may be cancelled later as the governing party changes. Wouldn't it make sense to involve the opposition more in the decision making, and to seek the common ground for the benefit of the medium to longer term? And thus prevent costly reversals on policy when the inevitable happens and the public mood shifts as a new government is sworn in.

Wouldn't a system that accepted these inevitable political swings that ultimately costs the taxpayer and public through inconsistent policies over a generation, be better served by one where a government shares the cabinet posts according to its vote share? Or receives a certain allocation of cabinet seats, sort of like a losers quota? Whilst the prime minster has additional powers to facilitate decision making and prevent deadlocks. People will ask, how will the politicians reach agreements? But then looking at politics as it is, they aren't doing much of a better job of it now as things currently stand!

Sensible politicians drawn from a wider pool of society and with a background in the government departments they are likely to work in, will be more interested in the delivery of effective policy in the long term interests of the nation rather than short term political gain. We can end the Punch and Judy politics that ultimately leads to the public switching off from politics; career politicians refusing an honest answer, choosing career over the public good and ultimately playing the game of politics. If elected office was limited to ten years for MPs, now recruited from a wider spectrum of society with more background related to their office, couldn't we develop a better breed of politician to represent us, that even if there were cross party differences, realised that the public good for the long-term is more important than any political game playing? And that by making an agreement to increase or reduce investment in the NHS, privatise the railways or not, raise police numbers or not, might be better decided openly among cabinet and shadow cabinet ministers from both parties with the national wellbeing the key factor, as opposed to voting according to party loyalties or influence from pressure groups.

Surely a better arrangement, allowing government departments to be represented according to the vote share, or having a 'losers quota' of seats and thus greater input in government, would be more preferable to a party that may have received 40% or even theoretically 49% of the vote from having any say in government or decision making. People all over the country would start to have more representation. Whilst being under the definition of democracy, our system in reality doesn't appear so. A sizeable portion every election regardless of whether the left or right wins, are left without a voice. Their anger spills out much later as the public mood shifts as eventually it always does and policies shift in the opposite direction, policy directives cancelled, new ones started and billions wasted. Surely involvement of the best and brightest from the grass roots up, leading to a wider pool from which to choose our MPs and ministers, would create better, more stable and intelligent politics to what we see now.

Each party with a sizeable chunk of public votes would have representation. Whilst MPs and the public will always have differing political opinions, it's the public who ultimately suffer when senior politicians are allowed to make costly and unpopular decisions that are later reversed, that could have been avoided. If there were a higher quality and greater choice of politicians for us to vote upon, and more MPs and ministers with real world experience, not in a job for life, under such a system we are closer to having a real democracy.

A similar scenario may be seen in the USA; Donald Trump recently elected in 2016 with 52% of the vote as president of the USA, but leaving 48% or so of the populace without a voice or representation. What if the cabinet posts there were also divided between parties according to the vote share, or a 'losers quota' of seats were allocated to the democrats to offer them greater input and assist in long term stability, and if there was a separate poll for the senior cabinet positions as opposed to being left to the discretion of the party or president to decide. We could start to see greater consistency in government. Of course many would say it's unworkable and nobody would ever agree on anything, but if we widen those involved in politics and change the way we can reach agreements within government, we can avoid the damaging and costly swings between left and right governments.

We might see a popular opposition politician serving under a Trump government, or a former general or Nobel Peace Prize winner who understands the horrors of war elected to overlook the Pentagon. What might seem far fetched now could be the norm tomorrow, we could reduce the bitterness and divides in politics that lead to stalemate, by inviting greater participation with the opposition party, voluntarily. After all who would have thought a TV personality like Trump could have been elected in the mainly career politician led USA? To one extent or another Trump broke the mould of only career politicians becoming president, that was a first for modern times. Why not have a new first and a new way of running politics? We would see a cleaner, fairer and more inclusive politics with more people involved at all levels within the political sphere.

CHAPTER 7

Greater participation in politics around the world

If in the UK, the USA and the rest of the democratic world, we can be seen to make a success of this new form of politics across the democratic world, then perhaps the rest of the world, sometimes with less democratic regimes, will be under more pressure to follow suit and improve their politics. What has been shown to be feasible in the UK model of governance can be exported across all democracies if people demanded it. Within the USA we replace the MPs with congressmen and senators. The titles may differ but the power and roles are similar as is the interaction with their party and business. In any governing structure; socialist or dynastic, with a fully aware public and the option of voting on the candidates entering the political fray, there is room for improvement.

As of 2020 there are around 114 democracies in the world, some more democratic than others. If eventually all the democratic nations accepted their inherent faults in their systems, the corruption, favouritism and party political instability, now much reduced for all the world to see, then perhaps those regimes in the rest of the world, maybe now not so sceptical about Western democracy, may seek to replicate a well-functioning system and adopt certain aspects of it in their socialist or dictatorial model of governance. Some commentators say that in the Middle East it's difficult to function with a democracy, due to the complicated history, diversity of tribes and religious differences within some nations. We can seek to make the system as inclusive as possible for those nations and encourage for there to be a wider proportion of the population working within the government.

Ultimately we want a system whereby a greater pool of available talent is drawn from wider society to enter and serve within politics. Since politics and its decisions affect us all, and the quality of our nations education, healthcare, productivity, security and more, are down to those decisions made by our elected leaders, shouldn't we develop a system whereby the best and brightest are drawn from the greatest pool of available talent? A system whereby every year new people enter the political world in some capacity, a world without career politicians, improvements could immediately be made to those 114 democracies. Surely those citizens of nations less free than ours can have greater voice to push for change if the inherent deformities in our own system can be seen to disappear. This is why both the time served for an MP, senator or congressman should be limited, and also why the public should be involved in candidate selection and not just the party. Therefore, the public not only have a national choice of which party to represent them, but should also help to choose the best candidates to run in the first place across the left and right of politics, the public now being more involved than ever.

In Latin America and Africa amongst others, often the corruption is more brazen and obvious but the same character profile of the career politician, able to be influenced and groomed by business or other groups remains, he may accept a briefcase packed full of dollars, a fee for a construction project. He may be part of a family dynasty where access to top positions are limited to outsiders. Why? Because the continuity of the pool of candidates willing and ready to receive bribes and seek power and wealth are assured in the next generation of politicians, by the wrong character profile of politician entering in the first place and waiting to fill the void. The top seats may only be available to those who tacitly accept bribes. In these nations change is ever harder but still possible.

Too often we see corruption and greed in the less developed world. How can a country expect to progress and grow when some politicians who do little or nothing for the public good, are all too willing to accept bribes and engage in rampant corruption? It cannot. How can public confidence in politics be allayed and improved after a scandal is over, and no doubt only a portion of fall guys prosecuted to take the responsibility? It cannot. Because many involved in scandals will live to fight another day and over time the same type of career driven and self-serving politician will resurface, particularly in the more corrupt governments of the world, that will be motivated by the trappings of easy money brought about by the endemic bribery and corruption, and the system to protect them after office. For some this may be motivation to enter into politics, for quick riches and notoriety followed by a comfortable retirement. After a scandal is uncovered and exposed, we may get a few years of relatively decent and honest politics, but media coverage is replaced by the new pressing issues of the time, it cannot be permanent, because the career politician with the heat off, will rebuild those contacts with new networks, protected by the closed network of inner government and media that will protect itself from public exposure and prosecution.

Sometimes it's endemic in the country's political structure that corruption will exist. Often a rite of passage into the higher realms of politics is the exposure to it and acceptance, which prevents that politician from having a free hand in pursuing his policies to the best interests of his people, since he is immediately opening himself up to blackmail later on down the line or worse, in effect, subservience for life to individuals and backers.

If political careers were limited, preventing institutional corruption from running rampant, with new politicians ready to replace the undeserving, there would be a regular check on government from the best and brightest, not just those politicians who see in a political career the opportunity for wealth and a comfortable career.

Sometimes an added benefit of greater involvement in politics is the safety benefits that it affords the politicians serving in the less democratic countries of Latin America, Africa and the Middle East amongst others. By limiting political office and breaking the dynastic tendencies sometimes seen in politics, it actually serves to protect those politicians from the harsher realities they may face, not limited to simply losing an election, realities that can be even more brutal. In an environment such as this, one can only expect to get the worst sort of politician if the decent and honest fear a political career – the sort of career politician that will engage freely in bribery, corruption and dynastic politics, the political rulers free to maintain the same corrupt networks and barriers to entry for the rest, that may ultimately cost them their life.

In the case of politics of some developing nations, we can envisage a time where, by having a limited career, and the public being fully involved in the selection procedure, there is a safer environment for politicians and greater participation. Now with more honest and dedicated politicians filling the void, this should improve the nation's productivity and allow the new breed of politician to operate in a safer environment.

CHAPTER 8

Expected critique and closing thoughts

It is inevitable when there are changes to our existing system proposed, that a move from the status quo will lead to opposition, many of those comfortable career politicians will be without a job, and corporate influence will wane. Who can we expect that opposition to be led by? Certainly the career politicians themselves who will be unstable in their careers with an influx of unwanted competition. They will say that the unique challenges in the job that they face means one needs to be in it for the long term, and they may suggest the job is not for just anybody, that they are indispensable, and their experience and knowledge over a career in politics is precisely what makes a good politician. But this is nonsense. In most other jobs nowadays, four to five years or even ten years is seen as a good long term employment. Why should the political world be any different? It's certainly long enough for a decent politician to leave their mark. John F Kennedy served only three years as president of the USA and yet managed to help avert a nuclear war over the Cuban missile crisis before his career was cut short. Many admire Kennedy still today and what he achieved, despite his short tenure as president, and seven years as senator prior, he didn't need twenty or thirty years to make an impact.

Opposition may also come from the media, lobbyists, large pharmaceuticals, defence contractors, any corporation or pressure group in fact that will have the most to lose by its inability to influence politicians, in the pursuit of greater profits. We can break the link between full time professional politicians and their cosy relationship with big institutions, think-tanks, and corporations that often work against the public interest. Those corporations that only seek government influence in order to allow them to circumvent the rules, win multi billion dollar contracts, get around loopholes, often against the public interest and in favour of greater corporate profits. The ideas outlined here can be implemented within our current Western democracies. Fortunately we do not have to seek a new ideology or drastically change from the system that we have. We just need to make the clear and concise changes required to enable the system to work to its full potential.

The intention as stated, is to involve a greater number of people in politics, whilst drastically reducing and ideally eliminating corruption and greed. That is not to say that a ten-year career must be the absolute limit, there could be rare exceptions to the rule, for example a politician after ten years may be called to the position of prime minister by popular demand. Some politicians presently are true public servants whether they operate across the left or right of politics. Tireless campaigners respected by many whether one agrees with their policies or not, they may be proven campaigners devoted to service in the best interests of the public and admired by the opposition. We wouldn't want a system that excludes people such as these from politics or even drove them out in the event that they had served their term if the public wanted them to remain on, as in the case of Theodore Roosevelt during World War Two who served a full third term as president in exceptional circumstances.

All that we can do is seek to change what we can now, before the link between corporate power and political control becomes too great and wide ranging for the public to change. In the UK and the USA at least we aren't there yet and so there is hope. We can slowly but surely envisage a better system, one that is run by the best of us; impartial and not led by decision makers sometimes fixated on a negative viewpoint against certain countries that we should be reaching out to for global stability, such as China and Russia.

So often the public do not agree with these policies, but by not having a say in the appointment process we cannot do anything about it. We're told you have a choice, there was a nationwide election, but the often hawkish chiefs of the pentagon, intelligence and foreign office departments are not chosen by us. They are selected by a panel in private and signed off by the president, generally by the advice of his permanent advisers, usually unelected staff. Despite politics shifting between the democrats and the republicans, that policy continues unabated. Can you find someone apart from the blinkered career politicians or from amongst those pressure groups and think-tanks involved in defence and war planning, that agrees with the recent flurry of wars since the start of the 21st century? The illegal Iraq war, the Afghan war, the Libyan and Syrian war, not to mention the covert and little known conflicts that seldom appear in the news. Perhaps only from amongst those appointed to the key departments like the Pentagon, precisely because they have a pre-determined mindset on intervention, or hawkish senators and congressmen who represent states that provide jobs for large defence contractors. These policies may run independently of what the president wants. The hawkish stance of these institutions rarely changes; the politician is given intelligence reports that support the Western narrative and often, with little or no knowledge of the subject, the career politician, now defence secretary, prime minister or president, accepts the judgement of the advisers whom he or she believes has greater knowledge. Often the cabinet minister, prime minister or president has no real world experience of the issues, or alternative sources to draw upon or assist them, from which to question the government narrative, making them easy prey to unelected advisors that surround them. They become in effect institutionalised themselves.

This is assisted since the career politician, through receiving campaign funding by those large corporations, is expected to be loyal and serve them to remain in a long job. The corporation, the campaign financier has usurped the public as to who the senator, congressman or minister now seeks favour. In a safe seat, what reason has he to worry about his constituents over that of his backers from whom he requires support to run every few years? Once in a safe seat for twenty or thirty years or more, he has no real need to appeal to the public for votes and can pursue his own, or backers' policies in a job for life in effect, with the focus no longer being on serving the public good, but serving and providing favour for those that put him there in the first place.

Deals and favouritism must be put to the dustbin of politics and promotion to key roles put into the hands of the public vote. Decision making on key facets of the national interest and departments that affect us most should be put to the ballot, not appointees selected behind closed doors in the interests of big corporations by inner government, to vote on policies that may be of detriment to the public, for example policies that may lead to increased weapons proliferation and more wars, or for a deregulated and debt burdened economy.

Let's begin a wave of change starting with the UK, USA and Western democracies to show it can work and then to the rest of the world. Let's clean up politics for the benefit of everyone. The knock-on effects would benefit us in every way imaginable making for a more secure, peaceful and profitable world. We would be a beacon for the rest of the world to follow; a light amongst the darkness. Let's begin that change today.